Giandomenico Romanelli

PORTRAIT OF VENICE

SKIRA

Front cover
Bridge of Sighs
Photograph by Luciano Romano

Back cover
St. Mark's Basilica

Editor
Eileen Romano

Design
Marcello Francone

Editorial Coordination
Carla Casu

Editing
Maria Conconi

Layout
Monica Temporiti

Iconographical Research
Marta Tosi

Translations
Liam MacGabban for Language
Consulting Congressi

Photographic credits
© Archivio Scala, Florence, 2011
© Dennis Cecchin, Fondazione
Musei Civici, Venice
© Emmanuele Coltellacci
© Alfredo Dagli Orti
© Matteo Danesin
© Hotel Bauer, Venice
© Hotel Danieli, Venice
© Jean-Pierre Gabriel
© Cesare Gerolimetto
© Pierreci Codess Cultura, by kind
permission of Davide Calimani,
Francesco Turio Bhom, Paola Baldari
© Luciano Romano
© Mark Smith
© Shutterstock

First published in Italy in 2011 by
Skira Editore S.p.A.
Palazzo Casati Stampa
via Torino 61 - 20123 Milano, Italy
www.skira.net

Printed and bound in Italy. First edition
ISBN 978-88-572-0960-9

On page 1
Giambattista Tiepolo
*The Banquet of Anthony
and Cleopatra*, 1746–47
Fresco
Palazzo Labia, Venice

On pages 2-3
Giovanni Antonio Canal
known as Canaletto
*View of the Grand Canal towards
the Customs House Point*, 1740
Oil on canvas, 53 × 70 cm
Brera Gallery, Milan

Facing title page
The Basilica of Santa Maria della Salute

Contents

Portrait of Venice

Giandomenico Romanelli
Director of the Foundation of Civic Museums in Venice

Today, Venice is a small city. But Venice was once a great metropolis – in proportion, of course, to the standards and demographics of its heyday – exercising far-reaching economic and military power and playing a highly important diplomatic role. Most of all, it dominated the maritime routes of the Mediterranean and many of the trade routes that linked the Western world with the Orient. However, what made Venice inimitable and unique was its "form", its physical structure, its architecture, its urban façade, and its artistic history and culture, which developed over centuries in a continuous transformation without ever losing touch with its origins and specificity.

Venice's appearance is so particular and so "different" that a photograph of Venice could never be mistaken for any other city, whether in the East or the West.

Venice, it is often said, was born on the water rather than on solid ground, and its roots are buried in the water and the soft mud of the lagoon. This is easily understood when we think of the first primitive mud and straw huts or the small settlements of the first centuries. Later, however, there were houses and *palazzi*, the great churches and huge public buildings. Nonetheless, the building techniques – though they had evolved – still had to contend with the marshy, unstable land: indeed the Venetians took full advantage of this, devising light and elastic building techniques which have kept the city's buildings safe from earthquakes and from the drawbacks and inconveniences that have dogged the histories of other cities. Consequently, today we can still admire monuments, *palazzi* and houses that may sometimes be more than a thousand years old, yet are still in use, despite their age.

Various legends account for the birth of Venice in such a particular location: in the centre of a precarious lagoon, forever under risk of being washed away or buried depending on whether it was water (from the sea or rivers) or mud or earth (carried down the rivers or brought by people) to prevail. The best-known account tells how a great invasion of nomadic populations form northern Europe or Asia (the barbarians) triggered continuous migrations as the Roman Empire fell. The inhabitants from cities and villages of Venetia, occupied by the barbarians, abandoned their homes and found refuge on the almost uninhabited islands of the lagoon. Here, they organised their lives and created a livelihood by fishing and producing sea-salt. This tale, however, is far too simplistic: in actual fact, the entire coastal belt of lagoons that ran along the north-western Adriatic from Ravenna to Grado had already been settled and civilized by Rome, with its own industries, farms, shipping enterprises, administrative and defensive infrastructure, religious practices and traditions.

It is true however, that the lagoon – the Venetian setting *par excellence* – was for centuries Venice's best defence against attack, siege, invasion and conquest. It is equally true that the Venetians spent huge resources on massive hydraulic engineering projects aimed at preserving the lagoon to the best of their ability. In every way, Venice and the lagoon constitute one indissoluble system.

In the early times, during the seventh and eight centuries, the lagoon area had been a rather peripheral part of the Byzantine Empire. It was peripheral but nevertheless strategic in resisting the expansionism of the new, former barbarian powers: the civilized and later Christianized Longobards, and especially Charlemagne' Franks. Venice was governed by military tribunes, nominated by Byzantium, who enjoyed a certain amount of political and administrative autonomy from the central Byzantine powers. By playing off this rivalry and exploiting their geographical position, Venice gradually began to acquire the features of an independent state, electing its own organs of governance, whose subjection to Byzantine dominion became progressively merely formal.

The election of the local governor, the *Duca* (later called the Doge), dates from the beginning of the eighth century. The name derives from the Latin *Dux*, meaning supreme leader. The Venetian State, a Republic, may be considered established as of the eleventh century (although it would not be until at least the mid-fourteenth century that the long process of establishing its institutions was completed). At the end of this complex evolutionary process, the Doge remained as the head of the Republic, but with considerably limited powers and a predominantly ceremonial role. He did, however, embody the unity and independence of the State. The great assembly representing the noble families (il *Maggior Consiglio* or the Great Council) had gener-

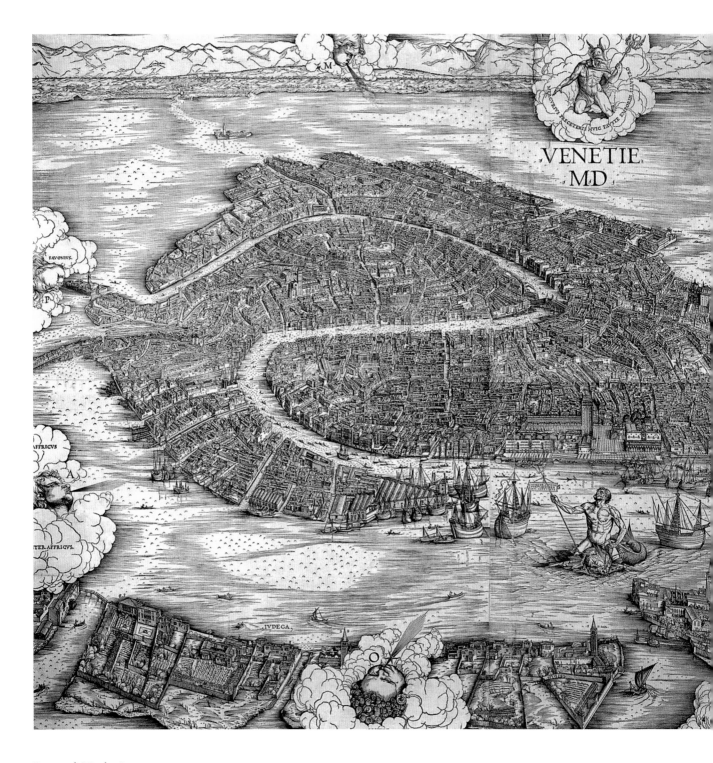

VENETIE
M.D.

Jacopo de' Barbari
Perspective map of Venice, 1500
Correr Museum, Venice

ic legislative powers, but did elect all State officials. A highly complex structure of magistratures defined policy and managed the Republic's administration, presiding over all the various requirements and structures of the State, the city, the territories on the mainland (the *Stato da Terra*, which eventually grew to cover the regions of Veneto, Friuli and parts of Lombardy) and the overseas territories (called the *Stato da Mar*, namely the Dalmatian coast and the Greek and Mediterranean islands). The Senate, the *Collegio* and the *Signoria* (the executive council) played a decisive role, as did, from the beginning of the fourteenth century, the fearsome Council of Ten, which was responsi-

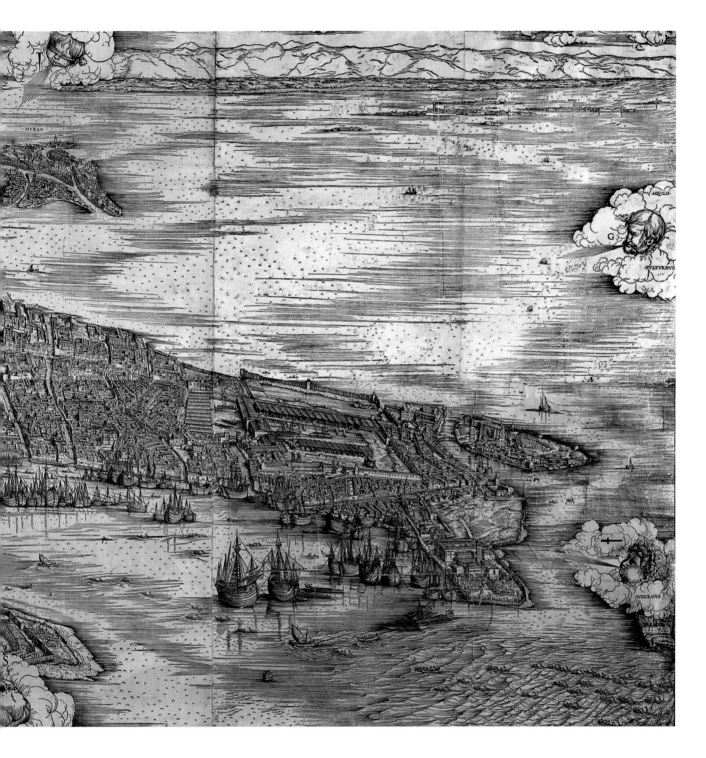

ble for all internal political decisions and State security, including the intelligence services.

The social class that held the governing power of the *Serenissima Repubblica* firmly in its hands was the *patriziato*: a nobility of mercantile origin that made up a very small percentage of the island population (between 2 and 5 percent, depending on the period).

The class of non-noble *cittadini* (4 to 10 percent of the population) was composed of professionals (notaries, lawyers, doctors, merchants…), men of letters, artists, architects, engineers, master craftsmen, teachers and the like. Among other things, this class ran the all-pervasive and efficient Venetian bureaucratic and administrative machine headed by the *Cancellier Grande*, a highly prestigious office in Venetian society. The great majority of the population (known as the *popolani*, the common folk) were excluded from any office or active political role.

A highly important part was played by the *Scuole* and confraternities. These devotional, professional or charitable associations united the members of one particular professional category or social or ethnic group (for example carpenters, glass masters, tailors, cobblers and craftsmen in general; later large and small merchants, brokers and transporters etc.) under a shared patron saint, insignia, sym-

the principal communication network for men and goods were the canals, called *rii*.

Initially, buildings were made in wood, earth and mud. The land lay mere centimetres above the mean sea level and the tide easily flooded the lower portions of the islands. It was therefore necessary to reinforce the banks, called *rive*, by importing earth, initially creating barriers of interwoven rushes covered with mud, and later of wooden piles driven down and reinforced with earth and rubble. Even the construction materials (at first just timber but later stone and brick) had to be imported from the mainland with considerable fatigue and at great cost. It was precisely the characteristics of this muddy terrain (encircled by water and often flooded) that forced the Venetians to devise a building method that started from the construction of stable platforms on which to set the foundations; though technologically updated, this system continues to be used into modern times.

Closely set pilings were driven deep into the mud and then horizontal larch planks were nailed criss-cross on their heads; it was on this base (called *zatterone*, large raft) that the first rows of stone were laid, gradually rising to constitute the aboveground floors. It is said that the immense Basilica of La Salute (built in the seventeenth century) rests on a *zatterone* supported by a million large oak pilings, and tradition has it that Rialto Bridge, built a few decades before, is supported by a much larger number!

bols and festivities. They provided assistance to members, widows and orphans in times of illness, misfortune or particular need.

And the city?

At the beginning, the city was made up of small groups of houses with courtyards, orchards and gardens, and vast pools of water (*piscine*: this toponym is still commonly found in various parts of Venice) for fish farming and salt production. The numerous small islands were connected by removable wooden gangways which were later replace by fixed, arched bridges that would not obstruct boat traffic on the canals; we must not forget that the canals both divided and connected the many islets on which Venice stood. The streets, paths and open spaces, called *campi*, were the secondary means of transit within each islet, while

Little by little, Venice began to take shape: some devastating fires destroyed entire quarters between the ninth and eleventh centuries (fire has remained a serious threat throughout the city's history) but such disasters also provided the opportunity for extensive reconstruction, in brick and stone. The first buildings to be erected with these "noble" materials were the churches: often imitating the style of famous Byzantine churches, or else elaborating on forms and structures taken from Western architecture. The monasteries and convents of various religious communities made a significant contribution to land reclamation and urbanization, draining and transforming marshy areas and building important religious complexes and economic and cultural centres on the islands scattered across the entire breadth of the lagoon.

Calli

In Venice "calle" means street. The main façade of a *palazzo* overlooks the water, the secondary façades and entrances, usually for the servants, are on the *calli*, narrow alleys haphazardly winding between the buildings.

Sotoporteghi

Often arch-shaped, these consist of a sort of tunnel that passed through a *palazzo* and link two *calli*, cutting through the very body of the building thus eliminating a portion that corresponded to the ground floor. *Sotoporteghi* are living proof of the Repubblica Serenissima's philosophy whereby the common good had absolute priority over private property.

Rii and canali

The waterways of Venice are an essential part of the city's network, the backbone of the navigational system. The small ones are called *rii*, the larger ones *canali*.

Following pages
Campi and campielli

The *campi* (fields) were the principal spaces of Venetian social life, where markets and fairs took place as well as open air public ceremonies and spectacles – indeed, the only space to be called *Piazza* in Venice is St. Mark's Square, an indication of its importance. The smaller, minor squares off the principal routes, enclosed by houses and not close to canals, are known as *campielli* (small fields) or *corti* (yards); here we often find wells for drinking water, identifiable thanks to the very beautiful wells in white Istrian stone.

Between the tenth and eleventh centuries the typical architectural structure of the *casa-palazzo* took form. Fundamentally, these buildings had two functions: an economic one, of warehouse and commercial office, on the ground floor; and as dwelling for the family and servants on the upper floors (one or two principal floors and, perhaps, a mezzanine). This scheme was derived from the Roman *villa* and the Byzantine *casa-fondaco*: a *fondaco* was a warehouse for merchandise, used by merchants in the various sea ports along their routes. An indispensable element was a direct porticoed access-way from the canal, which provided a sheltered area for loading and unloading the boats. This scheme can still be seen in many of the *palazzi* that line the Grand Canal and the other *rii* in the city.

The layout of these buildings included a large undivided central space on each floor (*portego*). On the ground floor, the *portego* provided access to the various lateral warehouses, and on the upper floors, to the various rooms. This functional spatial organization was maintained throughout the city's history, even after commercial activities had been considerably reduced or centralized in public buildings, such as the maritime and land customs houses or the general warehouses.

Over the centuries, this simple yet efficient scheme was dressed in a variety of architectural styles, but it never underwent any radical changes, even when buildings became larger and more monumental.

The dwellings of the majority of Venetians were simplified and miniaturized translations of this larger scheme, with small or even tiny rooms, wooden partitions and dirt floors; they were very poor and often in very precarious condition.

One of the great daily problems facing people living in Venice was water.

Being built on a group of islands in the middle of a salt-water lagoon, the city had neither rivers nor springs of fresh water. It was thus indispensable to find a way of collecting and storing rainwater. This was achieved thanks to the ingenious system of Venetian "wells". These consisted of large underground cisterns that were dug and made waterproof by coating its walls of in clay, so as to prevent the infiltration of salt water. Rain water from the ground and the roofs flowed into the cistern through ducts from the gutters and eaves: a filtering system, consisting of layers of fine river sand, purified the water to make it drinkable. The water was drawn from the cistern in pails via the well curb (the opening to the cistern). There were private wells in the courtyards and entrances of *palazzi*, and public wells in the *campi*, the cloisters of convents, even in the courtyard of the Doge's Palace. The carved white stone well curbs are an essential element of the urban décor; they are often set on a raised area that reveals the presence of the underground cistern. It was only at the end of the nineteenth century that fresh water from the rivers reached Venice, thanks to an impressive aqueduct built across the lagoon, bringing water from inland sources between Treviso and Padua.

Since the early days of the city, its heart has always extended from the area of San Marco (the waterfront, the basilica, the square, the customs house etc.) to the Rialto zone (the banks, the stock exchange, the market and the bridge across the Grand Canal), but there were also other important centres: for example, San Pietro di Castello, a small island at the eastern edge of the city, which became the religious centre and the seat of the bishop of Venice, known by the Greek title of Patriarch.

Work commenced at the beginning of the ninth century on St. Mark's Basilica, the doge's chapel but also an inherent symbol of Venetian identity. The church was radically renovated after a devastating fire in the mid-twelfth century, remodelled on architectural forms from ancient Rome but also from the "new Rome", i.e., Byzantium, and also on the Western medieval architecture of France and Germany (the style known as "Romanesque"). Next to the church stood the centre of political power: the Doge's Palace. Initially a true fortified castle, little by little it became a rich, sumptuous palace, where Venetian art shone in all its splendour. It housed the true power and administration of the Republic: the doge's dwellings, the Great Council, the various civil and criminal courts and also the prisons, administrative offices and official reception rooms. It was the beating heart of the city and the State.

The adoption of the evangelist St. Mark as the city's protector, replacing the original Greek St. Theodore, was an event of fundamental importance. The Winged Lion, the

Pietro Longhi (?)
Banquet in the House of Nani,
circa 1740
Ca' Rezzonico, Venice

symbol of the evangelist, became the symbol and flag of the city. Starting at the beginning of the twelfth century, the square in front of the church was reshaped. It was doubled in length and surrounded by "modern" buildings which housed all of the city's most important offices. The part opening onto the water was framed between two huge granite columns. Like the four bronze horses on the façade of the Basilica and a great number of ancient carved marbles, precious materials and artworks, these columns were booty from the conquest of Byzantium in 1204 by a Venetian-led fleet, whose real mandate was to liberate Jerusalem from the Arabs.

In the twelfth century, a large-scale industrial area was established in the extreme east of the city: the Arsenale. This was the state shipyards (however, originally it also worked on private commissions) for the construction of various types of vessels. These ranged from armed galleys for warfare, escorting the mercantile fleet or patrolling the Adriatic, to large transport ships, galleasses, cogs, round ships and galleons, which, in formation and under escort, periodically left the port of Lido loaded with locally produced goods and goods passing through Venice from all over Europe on their way to markets in the Mediterranean and the Orient. The same ships returned to Venice loaded with other goods that were either sold in the city or distributed to the other European markets.

At the height of its activity (a perfect description can be seen in Jacopo de' Barbari's cityscape of Venice, dated 1500) the Arsenale could produce up to 60 ships in a month. Several thousand craftsmen were employed in the various stages of shipbuilding (and it seems that under exceptional circumstances that figure could rise to an excess of 15 thousand). It has been quite reasonably claimed that the Arsenale was the first and greatest public industry of modern Europe, and this accounts for the great attention that was focused on it and the central strategic role it played in the Republic's economy (and its military and political security). Similar unwavering attention was dedicated to the maintenance of the Republic's forests, which supplied the huge quantities of timber needed for shipbuilding (as well as for the city's civic and religious construction).

The Middle Ages were a period of huge economic and political expansion: Venice was a leading player on the world stage thanks to its dynamic mercantile entrepreneurship, need for growth and sense of adventure. Marco Polo stands as perhaps the most significant and emblematic representative of Venice in this period, and he was destined to become a sort of witness and ambassador for Venetian culture as far as the known limits of the Orient.

The thirteenth, fourteenth and first half of the fifteenth centuries witnessed the appearance and triumph of a typically Venetian architectural style, which was actually a highly original interpretation of another development in Western architecture of that time: the Gothic style. This brought windows with a variety of lancet arches, elevated loggias, external staircases in white marble, and courtyards with characteristic decorated stone wells. The arched copings of churches were crowned with endless statues, pinnacles, steeples and light, very elegant elevated arches. Over these two centuries the city more or less reached its full extension: few large open spaces remained undeveloped and the glorious ages of the Renaissance and Baroque (the sixteenth to the eighteenth centuries) were more devoted to the rebuilding and remodelling of existing edifices than new construction. The sixteenth century was a period in which Venice established itself as one of the leaders in the golden age of Italian art: the Bellini family had already been active since the late fifteenth century, and the sixteenth brought Giorgione, Titian, Veronese, Tintoretto, Lorenzo Lotto, Jacopo Bassano and a host of other geniuses (and indeed the same could be said of sculptors and architects: Pietro and Tullio Lombardo, Mauro Codussi, Antonio Rizzo, Jacopo Sansovino, Alessandro Vittoria, Tiziano Aspetti… all the way to Palladio and Scamozzi), unrivalled masters of a magical artistic expression that was admired all the world over.

During the Venetian Renaissance, magnificent marble *palazzi* were erected along the banks of the Grand Canal, and likewise wealthy churches, monasteries and monuments, the splendid *Scuole*, public offices, banks and financial offices and the majestic Rialto Bridge, remade in marble to replace its wooden forebear (which can be seen in Carpaccio's paintings).

We have already mentioned Palladio: he was certainly the most important and influential architect of the High Renaissance and would also be the grand master of all European architecture until the nineteenth century. This was thanks to his works but also to the most successful treatise on architecture ever published: his *Four Books on Architecture* (1580) have been translated into nearly every language in the world. In Venice Palladio created some of sixteenth-century architecture's supreme masterpieces: the churches of Il Redentore, San Giorgio, Le Zitelle, and San Pietro.

The Baroque period also brought an impressive contribution to the city's appearance: the flamboyant taste typical of the age produced such veritable masterpieces as the churches of La Salute, I Scalzi, I Gesuiti, Santa Maria del Giglio and San Moisè; and *palazzi* such as Ca' Pesaro, Ca' Bon-Rezzonico, Ca' Pisani and Palazzo Labia.

Starting in the sixteenth century, Venice's maritime, military and economic power began to wane: the new international ocean trade routes and the rise of Turkish power in the Mediterranean, leading to costly and nearly useless wars, were the principal factors precipitating the crisis. But it was also the city's legendary enterprising spirit that began to falter; Venice's ruling class chose to invest in estates on the mainland, building magnificent residences in the countryside (the famous villas which boasted Palladio as their greatest and most original poet) and gradually handing over mercantile enterprise and risk to others.

Nonetheless, the eighteenth century was still a period of great splendour and success in painting, architecture and sculpture, music and theatre, poetry and travel literature. Venetian culture continued to play a leading role in Europe. We may think of such figures as Goldoni, Gozzi, Vivaldi and Galuppi, and especially Tiepolo, Rosalba Carriera, Sebastiano and Marco Ricci, Giovanni Antonio Pellegrini, Pietro Longhi and the phenomenal success of landscape paintings by Canaletto, Bellotto, Carlevarijs and Guardi. In short, the city continued to live, to transform itself, to produce, to dictate the rules of refined, luxury living, amid dissipation and folly in a sort of endless party, an eternal carnival: it is no surprise, in such a context, to see the world fame of a figure such as Giacomo Casanova, a seducer, adventurer, spy, man of letters, great traveller and *bon viveur…*

The eighteenth century, moreover, saw a growth in the production of luxury goods: fabrics, costumes, perfumes, footwear, lace and lacquers. It was glass in particular, already the city's handicraft *par excellence* during the Renaissance, highly original and kaleidoscopic, with its secret and inimitable techniques, to witness even further expansion: Murano produced decorated blown glass in the most refined and fanciful forms; Venetian chandeliers were sought all over the world thanks to their lavish originality, as were mirrors, either plain or engraved, vases, centrepieces, plates, cutlery and ornaments both minuscule and gigantic. The production of pearls deserves particular mention: these were used in fashion, decoration, furniture and jewellery and were shipped all over the world with great and enduring success.

After a century of excesses and cultural and artistic triumphs, but also of political stagnation and increasing crisis, the Republic of Venice dissolved and died. International vicissitudes were certainly the immediate cause, in particular Napoleon's expansionism and the battle for European supremacy undertaken by the great powers. Venice proclaimed unarmed neutrality at first, unable to decide which side it should take. It then attempted to save itself by buying off French diplomats. Finally, the Great Council proclaimed, along with the abdication of the last doge, its inglorious end: it was May of the fateful year 1797.

It was the end of a Republic that was once proud, courageous and triumphant, but had been incapable of enacting reform or keeping up with the times, and had been paralysed by the power-games of a ruling class that had lost its courage, purpose and dignity.

"And after that?" – this is indeed a legitimate question.
The end of the Republic did not mean the end of the city and its heritage of culture, history, art, traditions, creativity and taste.
In 1806 Venice fell under Napoleon's political control, changing masters in 1814 when the Austrians took over. It fought for its independence and to join the newly-born Kingdom of Italy, which it did in 1866. This was the beginning of Venice's "contemporary" history, which continues to this day. Venice's history after the fall of the Re-

public cannot be considered "minor" when compared to the previous centuries! Though no longer the capital of an independent state, Venice has preserved an important role: suffice it to think of the city's significance in the world of classical and contemporary art. Since the end of the nineteenth century (from 1895, to be precise) with the establishment of the Venice Biennale, every second year the city has hosted the world's most important modern art exhibition. In 1930, the first international film festival was inaugurated in Venice. Collectors and leading figures in the art world have settled in Venice: think of Mariano Fortuny at the end of the nineteenth century, Peggy Guggenheim during the fifties, and today, the François Pinault Foundation, and the list goes on…. In final analysis, Venice continues to be an indispensable reference point for art and culture, for music, theatre, dance, glass making, mosaics and much more.

We have inherited many problems from the past which are still unresolved, and in some cases have even worsened with time: the city's physical conservation, its defences against the water, the risks of air and water pollution, the difficulties of communications and transport, the ageing population, coupled to the high cost of living and the problems facing young people in seeking employment and affordable living spaces in the city. One can see that many of these are issues shared by many historical cities. However, they are exacerbated and complicated by Venice's specificity, that difference we spoke about at the beginning. Living on the water can be pleasant and original, but it is also costly and complicated. And yet…

And yet, Venice is a life-style "model" of particular interest for many scholars and observers. It is a city without cars, thus free of the dangers of traffic, especially to children, who can circulate freely within it, and also free of the air and noise pollution that traffic creates. It offers a less stressful and more human time-scale and life-style in aesthetically gratifying surroundings. It has an impressive endowment of historic treasures (architecture, open spaces), that can be enjoyed by all as places of public entertainment and collective events. Its many gardens and green areas, although frequently hidden from view, are noteworthy. The lagoon is a sort of natural park, and its various islands offer quality agricultural produce. Moreover, there are very fine antique structures that are waiting for attention so they can reveal their great potential: for example the immense machine that is the Arsenale (which occupies about one fifth of the city's surface area), the spaces of the Biennale or the huge buildings that are still available for a variety of purposes (the Scuola della Misericordia, many churches that are no longer used for religious services, and former industrial facilities…). Recently, some exemplary projects of this kind have been carried out by the city, the State and private interests.

The city is still, and increasingly, a precious and privileged place of knowledge and memory: museums, archives, libraries, cultural institutions, cultural and scientific research foundations. Thanks to its culture and art, Venice has stood as a beacon light illuminating the way for the entire world over long periods of history. It has been a place of scientific research and industrial innovation (suffice it to think of the Arsenale, where large vessels were built in a sort of assembly line capable of extraordinary output; or the organization of Murano glass production; or the weaving industry. Or printing: in the sixteenth century Venice had the largest number of publishers and printers in the world, the pocket edition was invented here). New financial techniques and mercantile instruments were devised and implemented in Venice (letters of credit, bills of exchange, insurance and risk-sharing), something which made Venetian merchants and their trade routes competitive, if not unbeatable. Even today, important universities, training institutions and international organizations keep these traditions alive, maintaining strong bonds between the past and the present and looking towards the future. Following along that same road, avoiding regrets and regressive nostalgia, there is no doubt that Venice can still be a universal point of reference, a virtuous model of civilization, dynamism and good, modern quality life.

The heart of Venice, the seat of political and religious power, has for centuries been the area around St. Mark's Square: the Basilica, the Bell Tower and the Doge's Palace. This unique civic space, which hosts millions of tourists from all over the world each year, has always been the setting of the most important events of city life, from the Serenissima's celebrations of maritime victory and the arrival of kings and ambassadors in the past, to the Carnival and other modern events.

Arriving from the water, one is struck by the imposing and elegant Doge's Palace, the two tall columns bearing the Lion of St. Mark and the statue of Venice's earlier patron saint, St. Theodore. Sansovino's Library, a masterpiece of sixteenth century architecture is dwarfed by the massive Bell Tower; to its left stand Palazzo della Zecca – formerly the seat of the State mint, which now houses the Marciana National Library – and the Procuratie Nuove, completed by Baldassarre Longhena in the mid-seventeenth century, overlooking the Napoleonic Gardens: all of this bears witness to Venice's extraordinary historical and artistic past.

St. Mark's Basilica

It's the city's most important monument, a temple of civic as well as religious life. The first Basilica, consecrated in 832, was built to house the relics of St. Mark, which had been brought to the city three years earlier, ousting the earlier patron St. Theodore. Having been damaged in a series of fires, the church was rebuilt from 1094. For over a thousand years it was the doge's chapel and was governed directly by the doge. Only in 1807 it became the seat of the patriarch and the city's cathedral. Venice's greatness was always reflected in the richness of its Basilica, which over the centuries was embellished with precious artefacts and artworks. The façade is adorned with mosaics, columns, ancient bas-reliefs and copies of the four bronze horses (on page 40), booty brought back after the sack of Constantinople in 1204.

TELIEXNOE9CESSASETÓ DUVIII:

The Baptistery

The Basilica's atrium, splendidly decorated in marbles and mosaics, was originally reserved for the neophytes, adults who had yet to be baptised and had to leave the church at the celebration of the Eucharist. The cycle of mosaics was dedicated to these new converts, and describes the history of the chosen people from the book of Genesis (above, a detail of Noah freeing the dove after the Great Flood) to the story of Moses. The Baptistery (left) is located in the south end of the atrium and laid out in three communicating rooms.

Mosaics

The interior of the Basilica, essentially an example of classical and Byzantine architecture, is a triumph of mosaic covering a surface area of over 8000 m². These mostly gilded images cover the walls and the interior of the five domes, creating an ethereal effect: they depict biblical stories, episodes from the life of Christ, the Virgin and St. Mark and scenes related to the most important Christian feasts.

The Tetrarchs

Alongside the extraordinary riches in the Treasure of St. Mark's, a collection of Christian liturgical art and Byzantine and Islamic goldsmithery, pillaged during the sack of Costantinople and housed inside the Basilica, we also have the so-called Tetrarchs, carved in porphyry and set into the corner next to the Doge's Palace, representing probably imperial dignitaries.

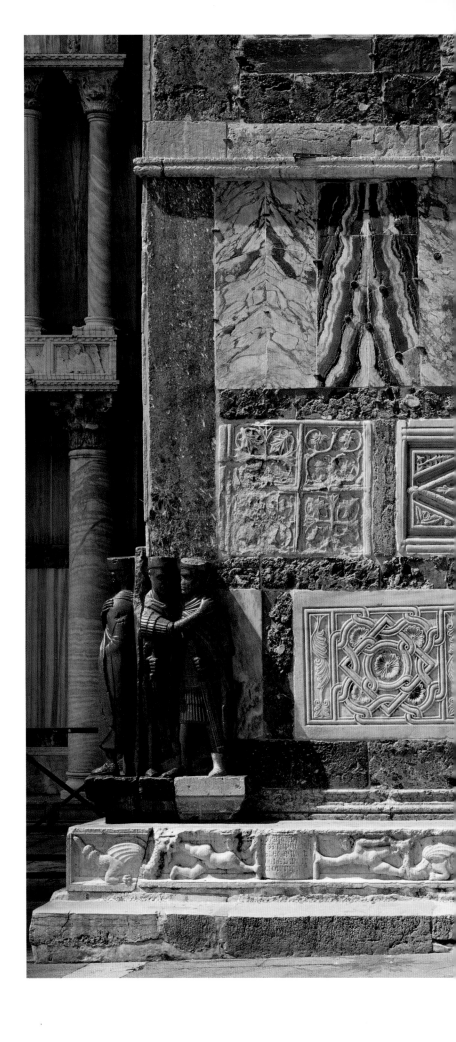

St. Mark's Square and Piazzetta ("Small Square")
It is the only square in Venice, all the other urban spaces of this form are called *campi*. It is enclosed on three sides by the Procuratie, called *Vecchie*, *Nuove* and *Nuovissime*, which face the monumental complex of the Basilica. The square underwent several transformations over the years: in 1807, amid fierce controversy, the church of San Gimignano was demolished and the Napoleonic wing was built in its place, uniting the two Procuratie buildings. Again in 1902, the collapse of the Bell Tower, dating from the twelfth century, temporarily modified the square's structure: it was decided however, to rebuild the tower immediately, "as it was and where it was". Initially a lighthouse for navigation, the impressive bell-tower is 97 metres tall. At its base is the Loggetta designed by Jacopo Sansovino in the sixteenth century.

The Clock Tower

Built between 1496 and 1499, the project was by Mauro Codussi. The clock, in gold and blue enamel, marks the hours, days, moon-phases and the zodiac. It is also fitted with a mechanism which twice a year, on the feast of the Epiphany and on Ascension Day, on the strike of the hour activates a Nativity carousel with the three Magi. On top of the tower there are the Moors of Venice, bronze statues so called because of their dark colour; representing two shepherds (or according to another theory Cain and Abel) they mark the hours striking a large bell.

The Procuratie

These impressive buildings housed the Procuratori ("Prosecutors") of St. Mark. They are divided into three wings that flank the square on three sides. The Procuratie Vecchie (on the right in the photograph above) stretch for 152 metres on a portico of 50 arches, to which correspond 100 windows on the two floors above. Construction of the Procuratie Nuove began in 1582 under Vincenzo Scamozzi and was concluded in the mid-seventeenth century by Baldassarre Longhena.

The upper floors, which Napoleon converted into his Royal Palace, today house the Correr Museum, the Archaeological Museum, the offices of the Civic Museums of Venice and a part of the Marciana National Library. Under the porticoes is the eighteenth century Caffè Florian. The Procuratie enclosed the third side of the square when Napoleon Bonaparte built the so-called Napoleonic wing, between 1807 and 1810, so as to complete the Royal Palace with a monumental staircase.

Following pages
The columns in St. Mark's Square

The column on the side of the Doge's Palace is topped by the Winged Lion, the symbol of St. Mark, the city's patron and protector. On the Marciana Library side, instead, we have St. Theodore, Venice's first patron saint. In the past, executions were carried out in the space between the two columns; a superstition of avoiding to walk between the columns persists among the Venetians even today.

The Doge's Palace

The two principal façades overlook the Piazzetta and the waterfront respectively. The "perforated" character of the double series of arcades, the portico on the ground floor and the loggia on the first floor, generates a superb chiaroscuro effect and at the same time overturns the traditional architectural equilibrium, suspending the monolithic bulk of the building on this airy base. On the western side, counting from the Basilica, the thirteenth column is larger than the others: it corresponds to the end of the Great Council Chamber on the floor above. The corner sculptures are attributed to Filippo Calendario or to Lombard artists such as members of the Raverti or Bregno families; they depict the *Drunkenness of Noah* on the corner next to Ponte della Paglia (on page 57), while on the Piazzetta side we find the *Archangel Michael* and, below, *Adam and Eve* (in the photograph on the right). The group on the north-west corner, near the Basilica and the Porta della Carta, represents *The Judgment of Solomon*.

The Doge's Palace, apart from being a symbol of the city, is an example of civil Gothic architecture, at the same time modern and monumental. Originally conceived as a castle, it became the sumptuous residence of the doges and the seat of several of the city's magistratures, and was the centre of the Serenissima's political power from the ninth century until 1797. Restored and partially rebuilt several times because of numerous fires over the centuries, the Palace was finished only in the seventeenth century, when the Foscari loggia and the clock façade were completed.

Bridge of Sighs

The bridge connected the New Prisons to the court offices in the Doge's Palace: the name, which may seem sentimental, is derived from the passage of convicted prisoners who sighed nostalgically seeing the view of Venice for the last time. In the background the Ponte della Paglia is visible, which links the pier of the Piazzetta of St. Mark with Riva degli Schiavoni, affording a fine view of both the Bridge of Sighs and St. Mark's Basin.

Loggia

The loggia, with its slender colonnade and ogival arches, is supported by the powerful arcades on the ground floor. The vast system of loggias that circles the palace conserves part of the original fortress. Like a truss of fine lace, the loggia's triple lancet arches and quatrefoil openings support the vast spaces of the *Sala del Maggior Consiglio* (Hall of the Great Council) and of the *Sala dello Scrutinio* (Ballot Hall). The loggia allows a sweeping view of the island of San Giorgio Maggiore and, to the right, the island of Giudecca.

Previous pages

Stairway of the Giants

For centuries this was the site where the doge's election was celebrated. Built by Antonio Rizzo between 1484 and 1501 against the internal façade of the Doge's Palace, in 1567 the stairway was further embellished with Jacopo Sansovino's colossal statues of Mars and Neptune. At the top of the stairway the doge was crowned with the *corno ducale*, the typical headdress, and pronounced his "Promissione", his promise to defend the Republic.

A Bocca di Leone ("Lion's mouth") or mouth of secret denunciation. These special receptacles were found around the city and especially inside the Doge's Palace; they were designed to collect secret letters of denunciations addressed to the magistrature.

The Golden Staircase

Built by Jacopo Sansovino between 1555 and 1559, it was the continuation of the Giant's Stairway. It is so named because of its vault ceiling, richly decorated in stucco and gold leaf. It was once reserved for magistrates and illustrious personages.

DENONTIE SECRETE
CONTRO CHI OCCVLTERĀ
GRATIE ET OFFICII.
Ō COLLVDERĀ PER
NASCONDER LA VERA
RENDITA Đ ESSI.

Hall of the Great Council
It is the largest hall in the Palace; here the assemblies of the most important magistrature in Venice were held. In 1577 it was seriously damaged in a fire. The restoration project that was subsequently initiated involved the participation of artists such as Veronese, Tintoretto and Palma the Younger.

Sala dello Scudo
The name derives form the custom of displaying the reigning Doge's coat of arms (*scudo*) here. The doge held audiences in this room. As well as the sumptuous decoration with maps the room also contains two globes displaying the terrestrial and celestial spheres.

Giovanni Bellini
The Mourning of the Dead Christ (detail), *circa* 1472, Sala dei Ritratti. A work that survived the terrible fire of 1577.

Vittore Carpaccio
The Lion of St. Mark, 1516, Sala Grimani. The symbol of the Apostle and patron saint of the city.

Giambattista Tiepolo
Neptune offers gifts to Venice, 1758.
Venezia, dressed as a late sixteenth century lady, sits next to Neptune, god of the sea, bearing a cornucopia.

Following pages
Paolo Veronese
The Triumph of Venice (detail),
1582.
The apotheosis of the city,
crowned by angels and encircled
by virtues.

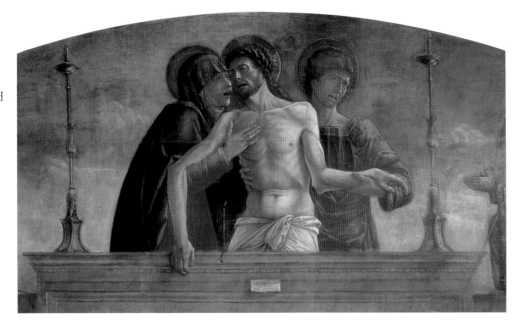

Paolo Veronese
Juno showering Venice with gifts, 1553–56.
This painting adorns the ceiling of the Sala delle Udienze del Consiglio dei Dieci ("Hall of the Audience of the Council of Ten"). Venice is portrayed as a young lady in "modern" dress, whom Juno endows with the insignia of power, the *corno dogale*, a crown, money and jewels signifying power. At her feet is the lion, the symbol of the city.
The Council of Ten was established in 1310, as a temporary body to respond to a plot led by some nobles who attempted to overthrow the State institutions. It eventually became a permanent body with mansions that extended to every sector of public life. The assembly was made up of ten members chosen by the Senate and elected by the Great Council as well as the doge and his six councillors. All these members are depicted in the seventeen frames that form the semicircle still visible in the hall.

Opposite page
Paolo Veronese
Venice enthroned between Justice and Peace, 1577–78.
This ceiling is one of the artist's masterpieces; it celebrates the Republic's good governance, the Faith on which it was founded and the Virtues that guided it.
The Sala del Collegio ("Hall of the College") was the meeting place of the Collegio dei Savi (or "Councillors") and the Serenissima Signoria, organs responsible for State administration and representation. Decoration was completed after the fire in 1574, on a project by Andrea Palladio.

Tintoretto
The Triumph of Venice as Queen of the Seas, 1587–94
Hall of the Senate.
The divinities surrounding Venice represent members of the Council assembly.

Opposite page
Hall of the Senate
Also known as Sala dei Pregadi, because the doge would formally pray (*pregare*) the members to participate at the meetings which were held in this room. The Senate was one of Venice's oldest institutions.

Ballot Hall
Initially intended to house the manuscripts left to the Republic by Petrarch and Bessarione, the room used to be called the library (*Sala della Libreria*). Later, in 1532, it was decided to use the room for counting the ballots (*scrutinio*), in the election of the doge. The paintings on the walls tell of battles won by Venice between 809 and 1656. The southern wall is decorated with a *Last Judgement* by Palma the Younger.

Following pages
Prisons
In the palace's prisons, known as the *Pozzi* and the *Piombi* (the "wells", on the damp and unhealthy ground floor, and the "leads", just beneath the roof lead sheeting), some illustrious figures were incarcerated, including Giacomo Casanova, Giordano Bruno and Silvio Pellico.

Opposite page
The Correr Museum
The collection that Teodoro
Correr bequeathed to the city
in 1830 has been housed in St.
Mark's Square since 1922, in
the rooms of the Napoleonic
wing and part of the Procuratie
Nuove. As well as an important
collection of documents, relics,
banners, costumes and arms
that testify to life in Venice
between the fourteenth and the
eighteenth centuries, the
extraordinary art collection
provides a well-rounded
itinerary through Venetian art,
from its origins to the Early
Renaissance. Above and on the
following pages, some of the
Museum's masterpieces.

Lazzaro Bastiani
*The arrival in Venice of the
Duke of Ferrara Ercole I d'Este
and his son Alfonso*, 1487.
The end of the fifteenth
century saw a great flowering
of art in Venice: among the
artists working in the city were
Carpaccio, Antonello da
Messina and Bartolomeo
Vivarini, Bastiani's teacher.

Antonello da Messina
Pietà with three angels, 1475 (?).
With Renaissance forms and
a compact, crystalline use of
colour typical of Nordic
painting, Antonello influenced
the artists of the Serenissima,
especially Giovanni Bellini.

Antonio Leonelli da Crevalcore (attributed to)
Portrait of a Young man, 1475.
Perhaps part of a marriage diptych, as suggested by the prayerbook on the ledge with the ring and pearl, this portrait is probably by Antonio da Crevalcore, a Bologna-born painter who worked in Ferrara. The fifteenth-century school of Ferrara strongly influenced Venetian artists.

Vittore Carpaccio
Two Ladies, 1495–98.
One of the most enigmatic of Venetian Renaissance paintings. Perhaps the two ladies with their wayward expressions are waiting for their husbands' return from a hunting expedition in the lagoon.

Cosmè Tura
Pietà, circa 1460.
Aware of the divine sacrifice, the young Virgin looks pensively down at her Son. On an orange tree, a symbol of the Madonna's chastity and purity, a monkey clings representing the basest human instincts, while the broken branch is a clear reference to the death of Christ.

Giovanni Bellini
The Crucifixion, circa 1453–55.
Light and atmosphere envelop everything, from the soldiers and the three men meditating on the mystery of death in the background, to the three dominant figures of Christ, Mary and John in the foreground.

Antonio Canova
Daedalus and Icarus, 1778–79.
One of the artist's youthful masterpieces originally housed in Palazzo Pisani, it is part of the museums rich collection of works by Canova.

The Bauer Hotel
It overlooks the Grand Canal, with a splendid view of the Church of La Salute and the Punta della Dogana (Customs House Point). Its elegant sixteenth century furniture blend with modern pieces of sculpture and works by Venetian glass-masters.

The Danieli Hotel
Only a stone's throw from St. Mark's Square, it is one the most renowned hotel of the city. Its elegant rooms have welcomed over the years many famous guests, among others Charles Dickens, Honoré de Balzac, Alfred de Musset, George Sand, Marcel Proust, Johann Wolfgang von Goethe.

La Fenice Theatre

Designed by Giannantonio Selva in 1790 for the aristocratic patrons of the Teatro San Benedetto, who had been expelled from that theatre; it was built rapidly despite controversy about its location and neoclassical structure. The theatre opened in 1792 with a performance of *I Giochi di Agrigento* by Paisiello. It was destroyed several times by fire and rebuilt. After the fire of 1996, it reopened in 2003 with an inaugural concert conducted by Riccardo Muti. Today it hosts an important opera season and the International Festival of Contemporary Music of the Biennale.

Santa Maria Gloriosa dei Frari

The Franciscan complex is immediately recognizable thanks to its immense Floral Gothic architectural structure. The majestic Basilica is the artistic and spiritual centre of the complex and it is flanked by the ancient monastery of the Friars Minor Conventual. The Basilica houses numerous artworks and has seventeen monumental altars. The tombs of several illustrious figures are also found here, including Titian's. Canova's heart is preserved in a funerary monument built by his pupils.

Titian

Assumption, 1516–18.
This grandiose altarpiece was painted for the high altar. The revolutionary novelty of the work officially placed Titian among the painters called upon for important religious commissions.

The island of San Giorgio Maggiore

San Giorgio Maggiore is today a venue for conferences and cultural events. Here are located the homonymous church (on page 89), a Benedictine monastery and the Cini Foundation. The island was donated in 982 by Doge Tribuno Memmo to the Benedictine monk Giovanni Morosini, who decided to drain the island's marshes. The monastery, where many doges are buried, became rich thanks to donations and privileges. In 1566 a decision was taken to rebuild the old Gothic church and the project was entrusted to Andrea Palladio, who also completed the monastery. The façade, inspired by classical ideals and the canons of the Counter Reformation, was finished in 1611 thanks to the initiative of Doge Pasquale Cicogna, whose bust stands out among those of the founders. The interior hosts canvases by Tintoretto, Palma the Younger and Jacopo Bassano. The island was abandoned in 1807, following the Napoleonic suppression of religious orders. It was Count Vittorio Cini who initiated the restoration project in 1951, bringing the complex back to its original splendour and establishing the homonymous international cultural foundation.

The Giudecca

Known of old as *Spinalonga* ("the long fishbone") because of its long narrow form, it was later named "Zuecca", Giudecca, perhaps because a Hebrew community had settled there (*Zudei*, Jews) or, more probably, because it was here that the *zudegài* (judged) were confined, people condemned by the customs court. It is made up of eight islets connected by bridges; the northern end is dominated by Palladio's Redentore Church (on pages 92–3).

The Redentore Church
It was commissioned by the Venetian Senate as thanksgiving for the end of the plague of 1576. The project, entrusted to Andrea Palladio, was completed in 1592 by Antonio Da Ponte. The church is characterized by an elegant monumental façade and a single nave interior with three chapels on either side, with extraordinary masterpieces by Tintoretto, Palma the Younger, Vivarini and Veronese. The lengthwise structure was designed specifically to accommodate the procession that concludes here on the Feast of Redentore.

Mulino Stucky

The imposing neo-Gothic industrial building that overlooks the Giudecca canal was built by Giovanni Stucky, a merchant of Venetian origin who understood the potentials of transporting wheat by water, a speedier and more streamlined means than land transport. After the entrepreneur's death, his son was unable to manage his weight legacy – rail transport also proved competitive – and the business closed. In 2003 the building was converted into a hotel.

The Feast of Redentore

Celebrated on the third Sunday of July, the Redentore feast recalls the fulfilment of a votive offering made by Venetians during the terrible plague of 1575–76, which killed about a third of the city's population. When the plague came to an end the Senate decided to erect the Redentore church on the Giudecca island and pledged that every year there would be a procession to this church across a bridge of boats, to give thanks for the end of the plague, a tradition still practiced today. A great fireworks display takes place on the eve of the feast, which culminates on the Sunday with the procession and numerous rowing races held on traditional Venetian boat.

The Carnival

One of the best known and most appreciated carnivals in the world. Its origins are very old indeed: the first known mention of the carnival appears in a document from the Doge Vitale Falier dated 1094. The institution of Carnival is usually attributed to the need of the Serenissima to allow the population, especially the poorer classes, a short period devoted to entertainment. Thanks to the anonymity guaranteed by masks and costumes, a certain social levelling was achieved and even the ridicule of public authority and of the aristocracy was permitted. In the eighteenth century the carnival reached its zenith and was famous all over Europe. The festivities open on the Saturday before Shrove Thursday and end on Shrove Tuesday.

The principal waterway of Venice, originally perhaps the natural bed of one of the rivers that run into the lagoon, it unwinds for about four kilometres through the city, from Santa Lucia, the railway station, to St. Mark's basin. On this splendid "street", always the commercial and transport artery of the city, stand some of Venice's most important *palazzi*, testimonies of its sumptuous past and today often the sites of great museums and cultural institutions.

The Customs House Point
The triangular form of the point, like the bow of a ship, separates the Grand Canal from the Giudecca Canal and hosts the low seventeenth century building of the Sea Customs House, where the cargoes of ships that arrived in Venice were inspected. The building culminates with a small tower on top of which is a golden orb representing the world, supported by two telamons and surmounted by a statue of Fortune indicating the direction of the wind.

Santa Maria della Salute
Venice was struck by several terrible epidemics of plague. During the 1630 outbreak, in exchange for deliverance, the Venetians vowed to the Virgin to build a church in her honour. In 1631, when the pestilence subsided, the Church of Santa Maria della Salute was erected, on a project by Baldassarre Longhena. This masterpiece of Venetian Baroque is built on an octagonal plan and crowned with a huge hemispherical dome; works by Titian and Tintoretto are housed within.

The Grand Canal

Also called the *Canalazzo* by the Venetians, it is the main waterway of the city and it winds its way in spectacular bends that draw a huge S, starting near Piazzale Roma, the access to the mainland, and stretching as far as St. Mark's Square and the Basin, in front of the Giudecca. It was the route taken by vessels since the Middle Ages, and it was once lined with mills, powered by the flow of the tides, factories producing wool and silk, and the old Arsenals. As the area gradually became residential magnificent *palazzi* began to

appear on the banks, mostly between the twelfth and the eighteenth centuries. These were the residences of the noble Venetian families: Ca' d'Oro (on page 134), Ca' Foscari, seat today of Venice's University, Palazzo Venier dei Leoni (on page 110), Palazzo Balbi (on pages 128–29), Ca' Rezzonico, the Museum of the Venetian eighteenth century Art, Palazzo Grassi (on page 124), Palazzo Dario (on page 111) and Ca' Pesaro (on page 136), which houses the Gallery of Modern Art and the Museum of Oriental Art.

Palazzo Venier dei Leoni
The palace houses the Peggy Guggenheim Collection, which can boast masterpieces by the leading artists of the twentieth century. The photograph on the left shows one of the sculptures in the garden: *Three Standing Figures* (1953) by Henry Moore.

Ca' Dario
Erected at the end of the fifteenth century, the palace is an interesting combination of Renaissance and Gothic styles and one of the most famous Early Renaissance buildings in Venice. Claude Monet was also taken in by the spell of this building, and painted its distinctive marble-encrusted façade in a series of works. The palace, however, as a reputation for being cursed, due to the unfortunate fate of some of its recent owners.

The Academy Gallery

This monumental complex occupies the prestigious building of the Scuola Grande di Santa Maria della Carità (page 111), one of the oldest lay confraternities in Venice. It also includes the homonymous church of Santa Maria and the Lateran monastery designed by Andrea Palladio. The museum houses the most extensive collection of Venetian art, ranging from Bellini, Giorgione, Veronese, Tintoretto, Tiziano, Tiepolo, to Longhi and the eighteenth century *vedutisti*, Canaletto, Guardi and Bellotto. The Academy has profound ties with the city, indeed it houses some of the finest masterpieces originally belonging to Venice's churches, confraternities and law courts.

Gentile Bellini
Procession in St. Mark's Square, 1496.
On the square, dominated by the imposing presence of the Basilica, is depicted the solemn procession which took place on the 25th of April 1444, for the feast of St. Mark. According to the legend, on that day the relics of the saint, in the golden shrine painted in the foreground, carried by friars under a rich canopy, miraculously cured the son of a rich merchant.

Paolo Veronese

Feast in the house of Levi, 1573. Painted for the refectory of the monastery of Santi Giovanni e Paolo as a *Last Supper*, the painting was the subject of an Inquisitional investigation due to the presence of elements considered irreverent. Veronese therefore changed its title to *Feast in the house of Levi*.

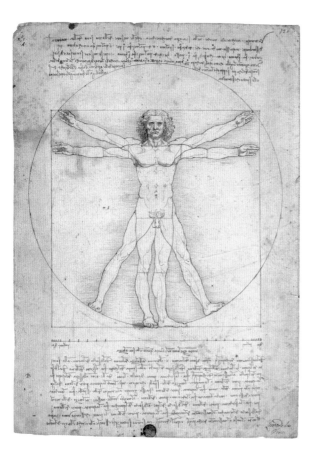

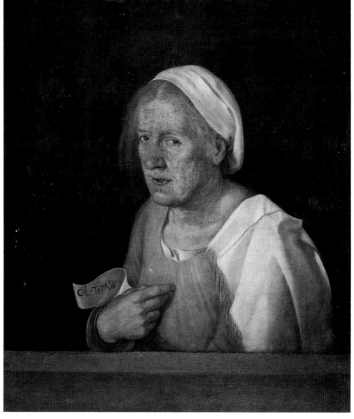

Leonardo da Vinci
Vitruvian Man, circa 1490.
The geometrical laws of human
physicality are represented here
according to the ideals
of Vitruvius.

Giorgione
The old woman, circa 1508.
This celebrated masterpiece,
clearly advising us to meditate
on the transience of beauty,
shows a woman, a wet nurse
or perhaps the painter's mother,
who holds a placard on which
we read "Col Tempo" (with
time), again a reference to
the advancing of the years
(however, the placard could
be a later addition).

Giorgione
The Tempest, circa 1505.
An enigmatic painting, thanks
to its Sibylline iconography
which has given rise to many
interpretations. Its modernity
lies in a shift from plain design
to an atmospheric use of
colour.

Bernardo Bellotto
Scuola Grande di San Marco,
1740–44.
This strongly analytical painting
presents a sweeping view of the
campo and the *Scuola* reaching
as far as the church on the
island of San Michele in the
background. Bellotto
assimilated in a very personal
interpretation the style and
descriptive clarity of his uncle
Canaletto.

Tintoretto
*St. Mark's Body Brought to
Venice,* 1562–66
This celebrated work, part of a
cycle of large canvases painted
for the homonymous *Scuola
Grande,* depicts the moment
when the Christians in
Alexandria save the Saint's
body from being burnt.

Palazzo Grassi
One of the last *palazzi* built on the Grand Canal in the eighteenth century. For years it has housed important exhibitions. In 2005 it has been given in concession to François Pinault, to exhibit his vast collection of modern and contemporary artworks.

The "bovolo" of Palazzo Contarini
Hidden inside a small courtyard at the end of a narrow alley off Campo Manin, stands one of the most unique examples of Early Renaissance Venetian architecture. It was commissioned at the end of the fifteenth century by Pietro Contarini to embellish the internal façade of his *palazzo*. A series of superimposed loggias connects the floors of the spiral staircase, called *bovolo* in Venetian dialect.

Following pages
Palazzo Fortuny
This old Gothic *palazzo*, belonging to the Pesaro family, was bought by Mariano Fortuny (1871-1949) and used as his home and atelier. The collection of paintings, fabrics and lamps is a testimony to the artist's genius and his eclectic work. The *palazzo* was donated to the Municipality by his widow Henriette in 1956. The photograph at the bottom of the page is an experiment by Mariano Fortuny, an esteemed and innovative photographer.

The Rialto fish market
This part of the city, next to the bridge, was always devoted to the daily green market and fish market. The modern *Pescheria* (fish market) was built at the beginning of the twentieth century on a project by the architect Domenico Rupolo.

...laco dei Turchi
...tes back to the thirteenth century
...s a good example of Venetian
...lle Ages architecture. Sold to the
...blic of Venice and later to
...te ownership, it was used by
... illustrious guests of the
...issima. Between the seventeenth
...nineteenth centuries it was the
...ish trading post. In 1858, it
...me property of the municipality
...ince 1923 it houses the Civic
...eum of Natural History.

...wing pages
...o Bridge

Ca' d'Oro

Built between 1421 and 1443 for the merchant Marino Contarini, it takes its name from the fact that some parts of the façade, that had a complex polychrome decoration that has since disappeared, were originally covered in gold. It is the most famous and refined example of Venetian floral Gothic. Today the *palazzo* houses the masterpieces of the art collection that Giorgio Franchetti donated to the State at the beginning of the twentieth century.

Vittore Carpaccio

The Annunciation, 1504
The Death of the Virgin, 1505–07
These paintings were part of a cycle with the Stories of the Virgin created by Carpaccio for the Sala dell'Albergo of the Scuola degli Albanesi in Campo San Maurizio.
In the case of the *Death of the Virgin*, the artist availed of considerable help from his workshop. Of much higher quality is the *Annunciation*, where the division of space is constructed around a tightly-knit geometric grid clearly showing the artists direct participation.

Andrea Mantegna

St. Sebastian, circa 1506
At the back of the portico Giorgio Franchetti had an niche built with veined marble walls and a fifteenth century style box vault ceiling, similar to a chapel, to house what he rightly considered to be one of the most important piece in his collection.

Ca' Pesaro

This masterpiece of baroque civil architecture was built on a project by Baldassarre Longhena for Leonardo Pesaro and his family. Ca' Pesaro has always hosted noteworthy collections of art. The last owner, Duchess Felicita Bevilacqua La Masa, made the *palazzo* into a modern art museum and bequeathed it to the city. Since 1902 it houses the International Gallery of Modern Art.

Gustav Klimt

Judith II, 1909
This is the second version of the same subject painted in 1901, it features a brilliant use of polychrome that recalls the splendour of mosaic.
The pervading eroticism is transfigured by the macabre detail of the severed head of Holofernes, whose hair Judith grasps with her long, elegant fingers.

The Ghetto

Campo del Ghetto Nuovo is the heart of this area. For centuries the Jews were not allowed to live among the venetians: the first permits date from 1385. The decree that established the Venetian Ghetto was passed on 29 March 1516, and it was the first ghetto in the world. It was created in an unhealthy area of the city where a foundry was located (*gheto* is the German diction of *geto*, from *gettare*, to cast, hence the name). It is divided into three parts: the Ghetto Nuovo, the oldest part; the Ghetto Vecchio and the Ghetto Nuovissimo.

Synagogues

The synagogues or *scole*, were built between the first quarter of the sixteenth century and the mid-seventeenth century, by the various ethnic groups: thus we have the Ashkenazi Synagogue (German and Canton), the Italian Synagogue and the Sephardic Synagogues (Levantine and Spanish).

Following pages

Ca' Vendramin Calergi

Between 1882 and 1883 the composer Richard Wagner spent the last two years of his life in this *palazzo*, where he died on 13 February 1883. One of the most splendid and monumental buildings of the Venetian Renaissance, designed by Mauro Codussi, today it houses the Municipal Casino.

Ponte degli Scalzi

One of the four bridges that cross the Grand Canal. The first project, of decidedly "industrial" features, dates from 1858 and was in cast iron. In the thirties the bridge was replaced with the modern single-arched structure, completely made of Istrian stone.

Regattas

The Historical Regatta is an important pageant and sporting event that takes place in Venice on the first Sunday of September. It recalls the grand cortège organized to welcome the queen of Cyprus, Caterina Cornaro, on her arrival in 1489, after she abdicated in favour of Venice. The cortège is made up of dozens of typical Venetian rowing vessels where the rowers are dressed in period costume, one boat carries the Doge and Caterina Cornaro herself. The procession starts from St. Mark's basin and follows the full length of the Grand Canal as far as Ponte della Costituzione and back.
After the parade a number of rowing races on traditional boats takes place on the Grand Canal.

Following pages
Ponte della Costituzione

The grand arch in metal, stone and glass is the fourth bridge across the Grand Canal.
It connects Piazzale Roma and the embankment of Santa Lucia, next to the railway station. It was designed by the architect Santiago Calatrava, and was inaugurated in September 2008.

The *Scuole* in Venice were secular confraternities, devotional and charitable associations that united the members of one particular professional category or social or ethnic group. They provided their members with economic assistance, employment opportunities, spiritual and material help in times of particular need. Thanks to their importance and the large donations they received, they had considerable wealth which they could invest to engage artists to decorate their lodges or in the cult of sacred images and relics.

Campo Santi Giovanni e Paolo
Known also as "Campo de le Meravegie" (The Campo of the Wonders), it is one of the largest in Venice and is situated in the area of Castello. In the centre, on a polychrome marble plinth stands Verrocchio's equestrian monument to Bartolomeo Colleoni, a military leader who served the Serenissima. The imposing Gothic church of Santi Giovanni e Paolo (or San Zanipolo) closes off a corner with the Scuola Grande di San Marco, which also runs along the embankment of the adjacent canal.

Scuola Grande di San Rocco

In 1478 the Council of Ten, the body responsible for authorizing confraternities, granted permission to establish the Scuola di San Rocco. When the association came into possession of a relic of their saint, it was necessary to acquire a permanent building that could receive the numerous devotees. In 1576, Tintoretto was commissioned to embellish the interior. In the large upper hall the paintings depict scenes from the Old and New Testaments.

Tintoretto

The Last Supper, 1578–81
The artist uses light masterfully, as the principle means of defining the volumes and the expressive elements of the scene, highlighting the most dramatic moments of this evangelical episode.

Tintoretto

The Adoration of the Shepherds, 1578–81
A painting from Tintoretto's cycle for the Sala Grande, it is characterized by a strong sense of narrative, a fundamental feature for works intended for catechises.

Following pages
Scuola di San Giovanni Evangelista

Founded in 1261, it was one of Venice's richest and most prestigious confraternities. When it received the title Scuola Grande, Pietro Lombardo was commissioned to adorn it with the elegant partition that closes off the courtyard. The main hall contains large canvases depicting miracles connected to the relic of the Cross, works by the finest painters active in Venice at the time: Gentile Bellini, Perugino, Carpaccio and Titian.

Scuola di San Giorgio degli Schiavoni

Founded in 1451, it bears witness to the presence in Venice of a large Dalmatian community, known in Venice as the Schiavoni. Venice's relations with this area intensified when it came under Venetian rule. Consequently this group felt the need to have a representative meeting place. In 1502 the Scuola became famous because it acquired a relic of St. George and commissioned a cycle of paintings from Carpaccio, recounting stories of the Dalmatian saints Jerome, Trifone and George.

Vittore Carpaccio
St. Augustine in his studio,
circa 1502
A true room of wonders, rich in carefully studied detail.

History of St. George.
St. George defeats the Dragon,
1502–04
In the painting, the soldier St. George saves the daughter of the King of Silene who had been offered as a sacrificial victim to a terrible dragon. The scene takes place in a peculiar landscape, scattered with ruins and macabre human remains.

The Arsenal

The name comes from an Arabic word defining a "house of industry". It is the first factory in the world, complete with construction workshops and assembly lines. It was the heart of the Venetian naval industry from the twelfth century onwards. The complex is linked to the zenith of the Serenissima's history: thanks to the imposing ships built here, Venice managed to vanquish the Turks in the Aegean Sea and conquer the sea routes of northern Europe. With the fall of Constantinople and the consequent advance of the Turks, the monumental Land Gate and the two towers were built, alluding to Venice's role as a stronghold of Christianity.

THE LIDO

The Lido is a slender island that stretches for about 11 km between the Lagoon and the Adriatic Sea. The coastline is characterized by the eighteenth century Murazzi, built as a defence against the waves. The old fort of Quattro Fontane once stood here but in the thirties it was replaced by more modern buildings such as the Casino and Palazzo del Cinema. In the central area of the island there is a wealth of buildings in Art Nouveau style and green parks (photographs on the following pages).

The main street is Gran Viale Santa Maria Elisabetta, a wide tree-lined avenue; on the sea side is the charming esplanade.

Excelsior Hotel
The opening of the Excelsior Palace Hotel in 1900 marked the beginning of a transformation for the Lido and a further opportunity for Venetian tourism. The building in Moorish style was designed by the Venetian architect Giovanni Sardi.

The Venice Biennale International Art Exhibition

The International Art Exhibition, whose first edition was held in 1895, is the most important exhibitions of contemporary art in the world. It is organized every second year by the Biennale di Venezia, a cultural society created to stimulate artistic activity and the art market in the city. The exhibition is held in the Italian Pavilion and the various national pavilions in the Gardens, and more recently also in the Corderie and other venues in the Arsenale.

The International Film Festival

The festival is held in the historical Palazzo del Cinema, Lungomare Marconi, on the Lido. It is the world's oldest film festival (the first edition was held in 1932). Its objective is to promote the knowledge and spread of international cinema in all its forms, as art, entertainment and industry, in the spirit of freedom and tolerance. The main prize that is awarded is the Golden Lion, the city's symbol.

Venice and her Lagoon have been declared a world heritage site by UNESCO. Nature dominates the Lagoon but numerous signs of human activity and history are also to be seen, which recount the story of the first settlements. Visits can be made to the islands of Murano, Burano and Torcello, with their traditional activities and historical and religious buildings, or else one can observe the aquatic environment, its countless varieties of flora and fauna and the unique Lagoon landscape.

Murano, the Basilica of Santa Maria e Donato

Founded perhaps in the seventh century, when refugees fleeing the barbarian invasions began to leave the mainland and started to build the first houses on stilts, this church, with its preciuos capitals and mosaics, is the finest example of Romanesque architecture in the Lagoon, alongside the cathedral of Santa Maria Assunta in Torcello. It was initially consecrated to the Virgin, but when the remains of St. Donato were brought here from Kefalonia, in 1125, the martyr's name was also included.

Murano
Glass laboratory

Murano became important for the production of glass when the Serenissima decreed that all the furnaces of the city be moved to the island. Furnaces had been responsible for serious fires in the city; concentrating glass works here was also helpful in controlling this activity.

A cup from the end of the fifteenth or beginning of the sixteenth century.

Following pages
Burano

The island is known for its brightly coloured houses, but also for the centuries-old lace-making craft (fine examples of this art are on display in the island's small museum) and gastronomic traditions.